Distracted

Finding Focus in a World Full of Noise

Eric B Summers

Distracted : Finding Focus in a World Full of Noise

Copyright © 2025 by Eric B Summers

Scripture quotations are from the ESV Bible (The Holy Bible, English Standard Version), 2001 by Crossway, a publishing ministry of Good News Publishers. ESV Text Edition: 2025. The ESV text may not be quoted in any publication made available to the public by a Creative Commons License. The ESV may not be translated in whole or in part into any other language. Used by permission. All rights reserved.

ISBN: 978-1-968112-94-3

Printed in USA

Table of Contents

1. Chapter One: Fear 5

2. Chapter Two: Fear Unpacked 13

3. Chapter Three: Busyness 17

4. Chapter Four: Busyness Unpacked 21

5. Chapter Five: Stuff 25

6. Chapter Six: Stuff Unpacked 31

7. Chapter Seven: Likes 35

8. Chapter Eight: Likes Unpacked 41

9. About the Author 45

10. Acknowledgments 46

Chapter One: Fear

Welcome to this new series, over the next couple of chapters we are going to look at people that we find distracted in the Bible and what we can learn from the distraction they faced. It's no secret that we live in an incredibly overloaded world. There are so many voices and images that come across our brains each day, and often all that noise causes us to miss out on the important things that God has for us each day. We get so caught up with the immediate things that we miss the important things. As we work through this series, I hope we can come up with some ways to be less distracted in life and have more meaningful interactions with other people we care about.

Before we get too deep into tonight's discussion, we need to have the obligatory definition moment. What does it mean to be "distracted?" Two definitions that you can easily Google are, "having one's thoughts or attention drawn away: unable to concentrate or give attention to something." And "harassed, confused, or disturbed especially by strong feelings." Being distracted in one sense is when we pay more attention to our phone than the road in front of us and we might end up in an accident and clog up all Main St. In another sense, we are distracted when we are dealing with the emotions that came up after said something hurtful and we can't think past those emotions for hours after the words were said. Sometimes we even choose the distractions to keep from dealing with a hard conversation or processing tough emotions. An example of that would be turning to a great book to escape the reality of a friend betraying you. Or maybe playing video games instead of spending time with your family. The underlying issue with all these distractions is that they blind us to what we need to do to move forward. They keep us comfortable or oblivious to what's really going on. In our effort to be 1% more like Jesus each day, we can't stand still. So, we must learn how to manage the distractions we face.

First, we are going to talk about how fear distracts us and hopefully come up with some ideas on how to overcome the distraction of fear in your lives. We are going to look at a familiar story from the Gospels and one of the Apostles particularly, Peter. Peter was an especially emotional guy and would often let his emotions get the best of him. In the story we are reading first, Peter asked something bold of Jesus and while doing something miraculous, allowed fear to distract him and almost died because of it. Turn to **Matthew 14:22-33**.

Jesus Walks on the Water

²² Immediately he made the disciples get into the boat and go before him to the other side, while he dismissed the crowds. ²³ And after he had dismissed the crowds, he went up on the mountain by himself to pray. When evening came, he was there alone, ²⁴ but the boat by this time was a long way from the land, beaten by the waves, for the wind was against them. ²⁵ And in the fourth watch of the night he came to them, walking on the sea.²⁶ But when the disciples saw him walking on the sea, they were terrified, and said, "It is a ghost!" and they cried out in fear. ²⁷ But immediately Jesus spoke to them, saying, "Take heart; it is I. Do not be afraid."

²⁸ And Peter answered him, "Lord, if it is you, command me to come to you on the water.²⁹ He said, "Come." So Peter got out of the boat and walked on the water and came to Jesus. ³⁰ But when he saw the wind, he was afraid, and beginning to sink he cried out, "Lord, save me." ³¹ Jesus immediately reached out his hand and took hold of him, saying to him, "O you of little faith, why did you doubt?" ³² And when they got into the boat, the wind ceased. ³³ And those in the boat worshiped him, saying, "Truly you are the Son of God."

This familiar story is the miracle of Jesus walking out into a storm on the water and His disciples being scared out of their minds. After realizing it was Jesus not a ghost, Peter asked a crazy thing of Jesus to the logical mind...let me walk out to you on the water. *What response did Jesus give to Peter?* "Come on" Keep in mind many of the early disciples were fisherman, they grew up on and around the same sea that they were up late fighting this storm, and it was winning. Peter in the middle of this storm asked Jesus if he could walk on water too. What was he thinking? It's a testimony to Peter's faith in who Jesus said He was, but it was also a little crazy if we are honest with each other.

Jesus had no issue with the request and told him to step out of the boat. With the wind blowing and the waves bashing against the boat, Peter put his foot out on water that should have immediately swallowed him up, but his foot held. He was able to put weight on that foot and then put his other foot down from the side of the boat as well. Step by step he got further from the boat and closer to Jesus...and then a distraction crept in. I'm sure he looked around at the waves and the wind and even though Jesus had told him to step out of the boat, that rational part of his brain just caught up with how insane this moment was. This wasn't how water worked, he should be fighting for his life to get his head above water, not walking out to see Jesus. And at that moment, when his rational brain reminded Peter that he should be scared to death...he started sinking. The distraction had taken its toll and now his life really was in danger.

As we read in the passage Jesus was right there to rescue Peter. He lifts him out of the water and puts him back in the boat. As Jesus hits the boat, the storm goes quiet, and the disciples rightfully worship Jesus. Nobody but God could have control over the elements like that. Before we get to the application part of the discussion, I want to talk about the short sentence that Jesus said to Peter as He was pulling Peter out of the water. "O you of little faith, why did you doubt?" *What was Peter doubting? Was it Jesus, or was it the miracle, was it himself?*

We don't know. But Jesus, being fully God was able to see into Peter's heart and knew that he had let fear win. I think I would have felt the same way given the circumstances that he was facing. It's easy on this side of history to point the finger at Peter and focus on his failure, when most of us would have a hard time taking that first step out of the boat. But in this interaction, Peter let's his fear get the best of him, and he started sinking. We are not going to be walking on water like Peter, but our fear can still cause us to feel like we are sinking in a situation, and the hopelessness is all the same. *So how do we deal with fear as Christians?*

You have all probably seen the IG reel or TikTok that says "Do not fear" is found 365 times in the Bible, one for every day of the calendar year. While that number isn't accurate, there are lots of times when the reader is encouraged to not be afraid. One of my favorite reminders is from **2 Timothy 1:7** where we read, "for God gave us a spirit not of fear but of power and love and self-control." Fear is not from our Heavenly Father; it's a weapon of our Enemy to distract us from what God is doing in our lives.

As Christians, we are secure in God's hands, nobody or no thing can take us away from Him. But the Enemy can totally make us ineffective for the kingdom by using fear. Instead of loving our lost friends like Jesus commands us to, we can be scared of what they might think of us and become distracted to the point they don't see Jesus in us at all. How sad would that be? We might feel like there is more God wants from us in regard to serving him at school, or on a mission trip, or even on a sports team, and our fear of failure or of rejection can cause us to just sit on that calling and miss out on what God wants to do through us in those circles of influence.

You get the idea; Satan wants us distracted from God's work and our fear is a powerful tool he uses to draw our attention away from what God is doing. We don't lose our salvation when we are distracted, but man we can miss out on opportunities to do amazing things. *How does a Christian overcome fear to be sure we aren't distracted from what God is doing?* In my life, I've found the best way is to lean into the promises we find in Scripture that God will never leave us or forsake us. Those promises have been true from the moment God spoke them and will continue to be true until the universe as we know it is done. So, when I feel fear creeping up, I lean on Scripture.

Chapter Two: Fear Unpacked

The goal for this series is for us to look at things that distract us from God. We are going to look at several people in the Bible that were distracted from what God was doing in their lives and hopefully learn how to avoid distractions and live fully in God's presence.

What distracts you the most each day? Do you feel like you could get away from that distraction if you really needed to? Are distractions always bad things in our daily schedule?

In the passage we just looked at, what do you think Peter doubted? Was it himself, was it Jesus, was it the logic of the whole thing? **Matthew 14:22-33** was the reading if you need to go back and refresh. Scripture does say one thing made Peter scared and caused him to start sinking. What was it? (The wind) *Can you see the wind?* You can't, but you can see the effects of the wind. Fear is that way too. You might not see a scary situation, but you can see the effects of that dangerous or scary thing in your life.

What is powerful about how Jesus rescued Peter? Jesus wasn't fearful of the storm; he had already walked a long way from the shore on the water anyway. He reached out and pulled Peter out of his fear and put him back in the boat. When Jesus put his foot on the boat, what happened to the storm? *How did the disciples respond to this miracle?* They worshiped Jesus. Nobody but God could do what they had just witnessed. I'm sure they felt fear again, we know Peter did because he denied Jesus after His arrest, but how do you think this emboldened the disciples to share the Gospel?

We talked about how Fear is a tool of the Enemy. *Where do you see fear being used in culture today?* Politics, school, families, advertising? Give some examples of what you have seen.

Have you ever experienced a time where you let your fear keep you from doing something you really felt God calling you to do? How could you have had the courage to do what God was asking you to do anyway? What is courage?

You can Google it. This famous quote says it so well:

> *Courage isn't the absence of fear, but rather the assessment that something else is more important than fear. -Franklin D Roosevelt*

The Christian has an amazing weapon against fear in the Bible. We have centuries of God's promises to us and not a single one has failed. We see scared people in all different sorts of situations and God brings them through the trial they were facing. What are some Scriptures you use when you are fearful?

Isaiah 41:10 Matthew 6:25-34

2 Timothy 1:7 1 Peter 5:6-7

1 John 4:18 Joshua 1:9

Psalm 34:4, 56:3, 27:1, 118:6

Proverbs 29:25 Deuteronomy 31:6

Philippians 4:6-7

These are just a few of so many verses about fear. In all of them, it's not on us to defeat fear, but it's God who does it! There is great comfort in that. Take a few minutes and make a flashcard of your favorite verse from above or another about how to handle fear.

Chapter Three: Busyness

We talked about some ways to combat fear in the last chapter, what were some ways you came up with? The challenge I left you with was to combat fear with the truth found in God's Word. We have this amazing book that shows us not only how amazing our God is but also that He protects us from all the things we fear in this life. So, you were supposed to memorize a passage of Scripture that dealt with fear. It's not good enough to memorize it like a test, recite it for a reward, and then totally forget the truth that God was reminding you of in the verse. You guys want to internalize these things because when life gets tough, you need to have a strong foundation to not sink like Peter did.

In this chapter, we are going to look at a different thing that distracts us from God and guys I'm going to be honest, this one I struggle with personally. Tonight, we are going to talk about busyness. When you get old like me and ask another parent how they are doing, the response you often get is "busy." Like it's a sign of success. If we aren't busy, then we aren't being successful. You guys probably feel the same way when people ask you how you are doing. "Busy" trying to juggle a social life, school demands, parent expectations, and all the crazy emotions of a teenager. It's a lot and it can be overwhelming. Even if you feel like you have a good handle on all those things, you may not realize how much of your attention it's taking to stay on top. Busyness for the sake of busyness isn't a good thing. We mistake busyness as a virtue in our culture when there are so many other cultures on this earth where busyness is seen as a vice, something to distance yourself from. So maybe we should just quit all the extra stuff we are doing and focus on being where God wants us to be instead of being busy...how easy is that to put into practice?

Turn with me to Luke 10 as we read a familiar story about two sisters and how busyness distracted one of them. We are going to start reading in verse 38. (**Luke 10:38-42**)

Martha and Mary

38 Now as they went on their way, Jesus entered a village. And a woman named Martha welcomed him into her house. 39 And she had a sister called Mary, who sat at the Lord's feet and listened to his teaching. 40 But Martha was distracted with much serving. And she went up to him and said, "Lord, do you not care that my sister has left me to serve alone? Tell her then to help me." 41 But the Lord answered her, "Martha, Martha, you are anxious and troubled about many things, 42 but one thing is

Jesus came to the house of Mary and Martha as He was traveling. These were some of His close friends. To get the house ready and be a good host, Martha was running around cleaning and prepping food. Mary on the other hand was just sitting with Jesus listening to His travels and teachings.

As the night went on, Martha was getting more and more annoyed with her sister for not helping. Finally fed up, Martha asked Jesus if He was concerned that while she was hustling, her sister was just lounging around. Jesus corrected her by saying what Mary was doing was the most important thing now. Martha had let her busyness distract her from God in the flesh sitting in her living room. In all honesty, I'm more of a Martha than a Mary.

I'm good at the logistical stuff around the church and focus more on making sure everything is ready to go and will often miss conversation opportunities because I'm busy. I see this in my own life and acknowledge it's something I'm working on. My family has always had a busy schedule, we live in 15 mins blocks, and while it may seem that I'm doing a lot for the kingdom with that kind of schedule, I realize sometimes my busyness is what pulls me away from time with God and time with others that He leads me to.

In the next chapter, we are going to unpack the danger of busyness and how it can rob us of our time with God. Remember busyness is not a mark of success, maturity is.

Chapter Four: Busyness Unpacked

In this section we are talking about busyness. In the passage we looked at from Luke 10, busyness for Martha was chores around the house to be a good hostess. What does busyness mean to you?

Of the things that make you busy, how much control do you have over those things? Could you step back from work, a team, or a hobby that demands a lot of your time?

Do you think God wants us to be "busy?" Why or why not? I used to think a busy Christian was a good thing, the more I study and the more I live, I realize a busy Christian is often an ineffective Christian. Perhaps God wants something more from us than just busyness.

When we are so busy in life, what do we miss out on? Rest, family time, time with friends, relationships, quiet times, time in Scripture, time serving others, etc. So why do we hold busyness as victory in our culture?

Look up **Ephesians 5:15-17**

"15 Look carefully then how you walk, not as unwise but as wise, 16 making the best use of the time, because the days are evil. [17] Therefore do not be foolish but understand what the will of the Lord is."

How does this verse tie into our discussion? Would making the most of our time include cramming something into every single spare second we have to look busy, or does the rest of the verse hint at something else? *Can busyness be a foolish thing?*

Sometimes busyness comes an of offshoot of our race for success in life, read **Matthew 6:33**

"But seek first the kingdom of God and his righteousness, and all these things will be added to you."

and **Matthew 11:28-30**

"Come to me, all who labor and are heavy laden, and I will give you rest. [29] Take my yoke upon you, and learn from me, for I am gentle and lowly in heart, and you will find rest for your souls. [30] For my yoke is easy, and my burden is light."

What do these verses say about what we should strive for in life? Is carrying the weight of the world on our shoulders something God calls us to?

Psalm 127:1-2 have a lot to say about busyness and rest.
"Unless the Lord builds the house,
  those who build it labor in vain.
Unless the Lord watches over the city,

the watchman stays awake in vain.
² It is in vain that you rise up early
    and go late to rest,
eating the bread of anxious toil;
    for he gives to his beloved sleep.

What can you learn from this passage? Our culture paints rest as lazy...is that how God sees it? *What rhythm did God set for us in the Creation account in Genesis?* There is a time for work and a time for rest. God wasn't tired on the 7th day, but He knew we would work every waking moment if we could. Rest is prescribed by God is good for our bodies. But we all struggle with it. *Why do you have a hard time resting?*

Busyness takes our attention of God by focusing our eyes on what is right in front of us. The task at hand, the emergency we are handling, the person we are trying to impress, the job we are trying to get. But when we focus on the stuff, we lose the One who gave it to us to begin with. God knows what we need better than we do. Do you think He wants us to burn through our lives, dusting relationships and memories all in the pursuit of stuff? **Haggai 1:5-9** is a passage we don't typically study in small groups but take some time to read through it and hear what God is telling the reader.

"⁵ Now, therefore, thus says the Lord of hosts: Consider your ways. ⁶ You have sown much and harvested little. You eat, but you never have enough; you drink, but you never have your fill. You clothe yourselves, but no one is warm. And he who earns wages does so to put them into a bag with holes.

⁷ "Thus says the Lord of hosts: Consider your ways. ⁸ Go up to the hills and bring wood and build the house, that I may take pleasure in it and that I may be glorified, says the Lord. ⁹ You looked for much, and behold, it came to little. And when you brought it home, I blew it away. Why? declares the Lord of hosts. Because of my house that lies in ruins, while each of you busies himself with his own house."

All our toil is in vain if we aren't doing for His Glory. That's not a selfish stance from God; it's putting things in proper perspective. **Deuteronomy 8:18** talks about the source of our provision.

On the flip side of the coin, is there a point where you can be too "lazy" and that distract you from God? *What kind of lifestyle would that look like? What would take your attention away from God if you were living life as a lazy person?*

So, what is the balance between too busy and too lazy? *What are some road signs that keep us on the right path?*

Chapter Five: Stuff

So far, we have talked about how fear can distract us from God and how busyness can take our eyes off God. I know it's hard to manage how busy our lives are. Hopefully if you can't change how busy your week is, you can at least be aware of the time you need to spend with God. People will often think the Devil is out to ruin your life kind of like Job in the OT. There are plenty of times the Enemy attacks us with big things, but I think a more subtle and honestly more efficient attack from our Enemy is distraction. If we are too focused on ourselves and what is right in front of us, we don't have time for God. Putting distance in that relationship is a tool of our Enemy and he's been using it for centuries. That's why it's so important that we talk about distraction and recognize when we are being distracted.

You guys look around during your day and you can see distractions everywhere. It could be the person on their phone scrolling reels or playing a game. It could be the constant need to check social media to be sure you aren't missing out on something. It could be the extra work put on your at your job because someone else didn't do what they were supposed to. All these behaviors are distractions, and all these behaviors happen regularly.

One thing that distracts us all is our topic for this chapter. This item starts to become especially powerful in the consumer culture we live in. We need to see what the Bible says about how "stuff" can distract us from God. It's no secret that Christmas is a special time of year, and you guys are already thinking about what you are going to ask for from parents and grandparents. You might have already sent them ideas from Amazon or some other shopping site. Giving gifts to the people we love isn't a bad thing, in fact, gifts is a love language for some people. But when the need for stuff and the chasing after it takes over our time and all our attention, it's become an idol in our lives, and it distracts us from God.

Turn with me to **Mark 10:17-22**.

The Rich Young Man

[17] And as he was setting out on his journey, a man ran up and knelt before him and asked him, "Good Teacher, what must I do to inherit eternal life?" [18] And Jesus said to him, "Why do you call me good? No one is good except God alone. [19] You know the commandments: 'Do not murder, Do not commit adultery, Do not steal, Do not bear false witness, Do not

defraud, Honor your father and mother.'" ²⁰ And he said to him, "Teacher, all these I have kept from my youth." ²¹ And Jesus, looking at him, loved him, and said to him, "You lack one thing: go, sell all that you have and give to the poor, and you will have treasure in heaven; and come, follow me." ²² Disheartened by the saying, he went away sorrowful, for he had great possessions.

You guys might have heard this interaction Jesus had before. The other man in the passage was called the "rich young ruler." As we just read, he recognized Jesus as something special. He called Jesus, "Good Teacher." *Is that really what Jesus was?* No, of course not. He was a good teacher, but He was also God with us. The man asked Jesus what was necessary for eternal life. This young man had all the stuff he could want, but money couldn't acquire eternal life for him so he wanted to know what it would take. Jesus quotes some of the OT law back to this young ruler and the young man was encouraged. He told Jesus that he had done those things since the day he was born.

If I was in his shoes, I would be excited because when given the parameters for eternal life, I knew I had kept them and was anticipating a congratulations from Jesus and affirmation that I had eternal life secured for myself. But Jesus didn't stop there. Since Jesus was God in the flesh, He knew more about this young man, than we do from Scripture. Jesus was able to understand the man's heart and motives, He also saw what was distracting this young man from really living for God. He calls out this man's issue in vs 21 where He tells the young man he is lacking one thing, sell all your stuff and give the money to the poor. Keep in mind, this young man was described as rich. If eternal life was purchased by just giving money to the poor, he could have done that 10 times over. *What was Jesus asking of him with this verse?*

He had to part with this stuff. All the things he had collected over his comfortable life, He had to sacrifice it all if Eternal life was to be his. Jesus recognized that this man's stuff was more important than his relationship with God and if that wasn't going to change, there was nothing this man could do to earn eternal life. Jesus was the only way and this man's stuff was more important. Scripture tells us that this young man went away sad not because Jesus told him bad news, but he went away sad because he had a lot of stuff. What started out as a real search for answers came to a crashing stop when the man was asked to give up something he held too close. His stuff was his biggest distraction, Jesus called him out on it, and he left sad because the stuff was his priority. I don't think people would label any of us "rich young rulers," but I totally think we still let stuff distract us from God.

Chapter Six: Stuff Unpacked

In this next section, we are talking about "stuff." Stuff can mean anything that takes your attention away from God. Activities can take our focus off God, we talked about that last week when we talked about busyness, but this week we are focusing more on tangible things. To start off with some good conversation, *what are some things that you collect?* If you can't think of anything you are currently collecting, what is something you collected as a kid? Do you still have those things? *Why did you like them so much?*

People do crazy stuff for material goods. I've seen people do all kinds of crazy challenges for money over the years in reality shows. I have also seen people almost run-down other people to get the perfect toy on Black Friday. Why is our culture so obsessed with stuff? Some people see it as a mark of success. If we have the right car, bag, shoes, clothes, collection of nice watches, whatever, it shows the world we have arrived. *But are possessions evidence of a healthy life? What are some characteristics of a life lived with a healthy balance of work, rest, and God?*

Philippians 4:8,11

"⁸ Finally, brothers, whatever is true, whatever is honorable, whatever is just, whatever is pure, whatever is lovely, whatever is commendable, if there is any excellence, if there is anything worthy of praise, think about these things."

"¹¹ Not that I am speaking of being in need, for I have learned in whatever situation I am to be content."

and **Matthew 6:33** can give you some hints.

"³³ But seek first the kingdom of God and his righteousness, and all these things will be added to you."

What does Jesus have to say about our possessions? We already got a sneak peak in Mark 10, but are there other places where Jesus teaches about our stuff?

Matthew 6:19-21,24 16:26, Luke 12:15, 33-34, 14:33.

Read **James 1:17**:

"¹⁷ Every good gift and every perfect gift is from above, coming down from the Father of lights, with whom there is no variation or shadow due to change."

What does this verse say about the things we have? Where does our stuff come from? From God, so do we need to chase after stuff all the time or trust in God's provision for our lives? How difficult is that for you? *Why is it so difficult?* Advertising, comparison game, jealousy all mess with this.

We aren't saying that you have to sell everything you own and become a monk living in an empty room. That's an extreme take on the passage. *Instead, what are some ways you can either use your stuff for the Kingdom, or scale back your stuff and help others at the same time?*

How can we be content with what we have, knowing it's what God has provided for us? What is working against us in finding contentment?

Sometimes it's not just the stuff that pulls us away from God, but the pursuit of it as well. Sometimes it's the work hours we keep that keep us from spending time with God. Sometimes we sacrifice time with friends to wait in line for a new shoe release or the newest iPhone. In those situations, and plenty of others, the pursuit of stuff can distract us from God and His plans for our life. Have you ever experienced a time when the pursuit of something cost you time with friends, family, or with God? Jesus tells a parable about different hearts in **Luke 8**. In **vs 7** He talks about a type of seed that gets choked out by the weeds around it, in **vs 14** He explains what kind of heart that is. Why do you think the kind of heart mentioned in vs 14 doesn't produce spiritual fruit?

How can we be sure our hearts aren't choked out by the stuff in this life and the pursuit of possessions?

Chapter Seven: Likes

There are lots of other distractions when it comes to our relationship with God. We could probably spend an entire year walking through them all, thankfully we have had some great conversations about these topics, and it gives me hope that you will be able to recognize when something is distracting you from God in the future.

In this chapter, we wrap up with a topic that can take two different directions depending on where you are in life. The big topic will be how "Likes" distract us from God. I'm not talking about your likes on social media here, I'm talking about the basic human psychological need to be liked. For many of you, that's as far as the conversation needs to go. Having friends that like you, not being picked on by other people, and feeling like you have a tribe of people you belong with are big deals. If we don't have those needs met, it can distract us from God because we want the approval of physical people we can see and laugh with each day.

There is a deeper application to this topic as well, for some of you, being liked by someone has moved into more of a romantic idea than just a friendship idea and then the distraction from God only multiplies. In fact, there are plenty of people that get so distracted with the person they are dating or pursuing, that they not only lose focus on God, but they also lose focus on all their friends too. We will address both in this section.

As always, we are going to start with Scripture about each direction before we split off into groups. Let's look first at an example someone who kept his eyes on God even when others didn't like him because of that. Turn with me to **Daniel 6**. Daniel had been taken into captivity and as part of this country's approach to captive lands, they would bring in some of the young people from the captured nation and educate them and give them positions of authority as a way of keeping them from revolting.

Daniel was one of those and he had been given a lot of responsibility in the new land. It made some of the other rulers mad that Daniel was as successful as he was, so they started plotting against him. They didn't realize that Daniel was successful because God was using him for His plan. They realized the only way they could find an issue with Daniel was to make one around his faith, so they went to the king and asked for a bogus law about worship to be passed that they knew Daniel would have to break because of his beliefs. When the law was passed, Daniel could have gone with the flow, but he didn't. He cared more about what God thought about him than what other people did. Let's read **Daniel 6:14-22** and see how it worked out.

"**14** Then the king, when he heard these words, was much distressed and set his mind to deliver Daniel. And he labored till the sun went down to rescue him. **15** Then these men came by agreement to the king and said to the king, "Know, O king, that it is a law of the Medes and Persians that no injunction or ordinance that the king establishes can be changed."

16 Then the king commanded, and Daniel was brought and cast into the den of lions. The king declared to Daniel, "May your God, whom you serve continually, deliver you!" **17** And a stone was brought and laid on the mouth of the den, and the king sealed it with his own signet and with the signet of his lords, that nothing might be changed concerning Daniel. **18** Then the king went to his palace and spent the night fasting; no diversions were brought to him, and sleep fled from him.

19 Then, at break of day, the king arose and went in haste to the den of lions. **20** As he came near to the den where Daniel was, he cried out in a tone of anguish. The king declared to Daniel, "O Daniel, servant of the living God, has your God, whom you serve continually, been able to deliver you from the lions?" **21** Then Daniel said to the king, "O king, live forever! **22** My God sent his angel and shut the lions' mouths, and they have not harmed me, because I was found blameless before him; and also, before you, O king, I have done no harm."

Not only was Daniel spared from the lions, the kings love for Daniel was made evident in how he reacted to the sentence he had to pass. This probably only made the other rulers angrier. But the king recognized that the God Daniel was serving was on a different level than the false gods of the people and Daniel was able to use this whole interaction to introduce the king to the One True God, the God of Daniel.

As for when our being liked turns to a more romantic thing, we can think of David and a huge mistake that he made at the height of his power. David was the king, he had control of everything, as his armies were away at war, David took a walk on the rooftop of the palace to look out over the city. David let his eyes wander to the beautiful wife of his commander Uriah. David let his lust get the better of him and he slept with Uriah's wife. He tried to cover it up by having Uriah come back from war, but he refused to go home while his men were deployed, he was a solid soldier. After that didn't work, David sent Uriah back with a decree from the King. Uriah didn't know it because it was sealed, but it was to Uriah's commander that in the heat of the battle, they were to retreat and leave Uriah all by himself in the middle of the battle so he would be killed.

This all happened in **2 Samuel 11**. But where David's sin was brought to life was by the prophet Nathan in **2 Samuel 12**, let's read the end of the story Nathan tells to convict David of this horrible deed.
2 Samuel 12:5-9.

"**5** Then David's anger was greatly kindled against the man, and he said to Nathan, "As the Lord lives, the man who has done this deserves to die, **6** and he shall restore the lamb fourfold, because he did this thing, and because he had no pity."

7 Nathan said to David, "You are the man! Thus says the Lord, the God of Israel, 'I anointed you king over Israel, and I delivered you out of the hand of Saul. **8** And I gave you your master's house and your master's wives into your arms and gave you the house of Israel and of Judah. And if this were too little, I would add to you as much more. **9** Why have you despised the word of the Lord, to do what is evil in his sight? You have struck down Uriah the Hittite with the sword and have taken his wife to be your wife and have killed him with the sword of the Ammonites."

David was furious at the man in the story that Nathan made up, he was too blind to see that he was that man. Nathan had to tell him directly. David had been so caught up in his lust not only did he mess up with Bathsheba, but in his distracted state he had Uriah murdered in battle. God reminded David that He had given David everything he could have possibly wanted and would have even given him more if he had asked, but instead, David went after what he wanted with his own hands in a horrible way and look how it played out. This is a very extreme example of someone letting their like and then their lust distract them from God, but people still hurt their families, friends, and other families with their lust today.

Chapter Eight: Likes Unpacked

Being liked is at the core of our basic needs. There are times when our desire to be liked, or what we are willing to do to be liked will distract us from God. *Have you ever compromised on something to be liked by someone else? Was the trade worth it?* Knowing what you do on this side of history, would you make that compromise again? **Galatians 1:10** speaks to our desire to please other people versus our identity in Christ.

"¹⁰ For am I now seeking the approval of man, or of God? Or am I trying to please man? If I were still trying to please man, I would not be a servant of Christ."

How hard is it to live this out?

Here are some guidelines on being liked but not letting it distract you from God.

Be Authentic, show more gentleness (**Colossians 4:5-6**), be aware of other people's love languages, don't be judgmental (**Matthew 7:2**), be eager to help others with needs they have, love God more than being liked by people. *Which one is the easiest for you to put into practice and which one will require the most sacrifice? Why is the hard one so hard for you to live out? What can* *you do this week to get better at that aspect? Who will hold you accountable to that action?*

Let's go into a deeper aspect where our being liked connects to all kinds of other messy emotions as we introduce romantic feelings into the conversation. This will be awkward, but I have seen so many people fall away from their faith because of a bad relationship or they lose themselves trying to hold on to a relationship that wasn't honoring God.

In David's example, what distracted him from all the good that God had done for him and all the things God had blessed David with? A woman in a bathtub. Daivd allowed his lust to distract him from God and a terrible price was paid. Not only did Uriah die by David's decree, but the baby born of the adulterous relationship died as well, and David's family had drama until the end of his days because of this bad choice.

In the thick of the emotions, it's hard to realize that you are being distracted from your walk with God by a relationship or the pursuit of one, *what are some resources you have or would like to have to keep you focused on God in this season of life?* **Proverbs 11:14,**

19:20-21, 1 Corinthians 15:33, James 1:5, Galatians 6:2,

A warning that we should always keep close to our minds and hearts is found in **Proverbs 4:23**.

"Keep your heart with all vigilance,
     for from it flow the springs of life."

How does this verse connect to our relationships, and then how does it keep us from being distracted by that significant other? Do you feel like your friends are keeping God in the picture as they pursue dating? *Why do you think church and dating typically stay away from each other? How can we do a better job preparing believers to date in a way that keeps their eyes on Jesus?*

DON'T LET THE NOISE OF FEAR, BUSYNESS, STUFF, OR THE NEED TO BE LIKED DROWN OUT THE VOICE OF GOD IN YOUR LIFE. STAY FOCUSED, STAY FAITHFUL, AND TAKE ONE STEP EACH DAY TO FIX YOUR EYES ON JESUS—NO MATTER WHAT TRIES TO PULL YOU AWAY.

About the Author

Eric Summers has served as a dedicated student pastor for over 20 years, walking alongside young people as they navigate faith, life, and purpose. Beyond the church walls, Eric is a committed husband and the proud father of three amazing children who continually inspire and challenge him to lead by example. An avid soccer coach and lifelong athlete, he brings the same energy and discipline to the field as he does to ministry. Eric is also an active member of the F3 fitness community and a passionate rucker, always pushing himself and others to grow stronger—physically, mentally, and spiritually. Whether in the locker room, on the trail, or at the pulpit, Eric leads with heart, humility, and an unshakable belief in the power of **functional faith**.

Acknowledgments

First and foremost, I thank God for the gift of Jesus—my Savior, my strength, and the foundation of everything I am and everything I do. May this book help me push aside the distractions of this world and sit at your feet more readily.

To my incredible wife and our amazing children—thank you for your unwavering love, patience, and support. You are my greatest blessing and constant reminder of God's goodness.

I'm deeply grateful for the many mentors who have poured into my life over the years. Your wisdom, honesty, and willingness to challenge me have sharpened me in ways I'll never fully be able to repay. You've shaped the man, leader, and follower of Christ I am today.

And to my F3 brothers—those I meet with in the gloom—thank you for pushing me to be better, stronger, and more faithful in every area of life. Your accountability and camaraderie are gifts I never take for granted.

www.ingramcontent.com/pod-product-compliance
Lightning Source LLC
Chambersburg PA
CBHW071724290326
41933CB00052B/3112